Needle Crafts 11

KNITTING

GW00786494

SEARCH PRESS
Tunbridge Wells

Introduction

The history of knitting is obscure, but examples have been found dating from the ancient Egyptians. Along with weaving it is certainly one of man's earliest methods of making fabric. Like a great many crafts it was spread across the known world by the Crusaders and possibly, sailors. Fishing villages in many countries had a great tradition of knitting; each village had its own special stitches so that the body of any fisherman washed ashore could be identified by his jersey. In fact, the names Jersey and Guernsey are also the names of particular kinds of fisherman's garments.

The early Victorians were legally obliged to teach their children, both girls and boys, to knit. Today, however, although the bread-and-butter aspect of providing warm garments is still an important part of knitting, it has also developed into something of an art form. Knitted fashion garments, even to couture level, are showing more and more imagination but knitting is also used in wall hangings and other purely decorative items.

In this book you will find basic knitting techniques which provide the necessary grounding for anyone who then wishes to go on to the more advanced stages of the craft.

Fig. 1. Wool and needles

Materials and equipment

The necessary equipment, as shown in Fig. 1, is very simple and a collection can be built up gradually.

Needles
These usually come in pairs, or sets of 4 for circular knitting and vary in thickness enormously. Choose the size of needle according to the yarn being used.

Yarn
This ranges in thickness from very fine and smooth to thick and nubbly and is either natural or manmade. The thickness of traditional yarns is often defined by the term 'ply'. Basically, a 2-ply yarn consists of two threads twisted together, a 3-ply yarn three threads and so on. The higher the ply number, the thicker the yarn. After 4-ply, the terms double knitting (double 4-ply), double double knitting, quick knit and other non-generic terms are more usual.

Other requirements include a tape-measure, ruler, pins, scissors, a blunt-ended wool needle, paper, pencil and stitch holders. A needle gauge and row counter are also useful.

How to begin

Hold the needle holding the stitches in the left hand and hold the working needle and the yarn in the right hand. Control the yarn by winding it round the fingers of the right hand as shown in Fig. 2.

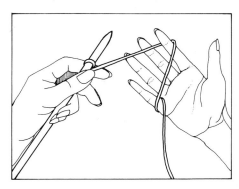

Fig. 2. Controlling the yarn tension

Casting on

There are several methods of casting on; the correct choice depends on the type of fabric. The method given in Figs. 3 to 7 is the most commonly-used.

Figs. 3 and 4 show how to make a slip loop at about 15 cm (6 in.) from the end of the yarn and tighten it on to the left-hand needle. Insert the right-hand needle into the front of the loop, left to right, wind the yarn round the right-hand needle point and draw it through to the front as in Figs. 5 and 6. Transfer the loop from the right-hand needle to the left-hand needle. Continue in this way, but insert the needle *between* the stitches on the left-hand needle, as in Fig. 7, until you have the correct number of stitches.

Fig. 5.

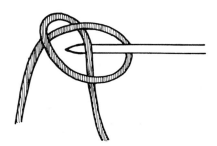

Fig. 3. Casting on

Fig. 6.

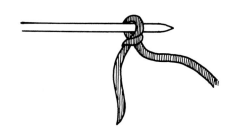

Fig. 4.

Fig. 7.

above:
Landscape with pylons. *This is worked in plain knitting and the main pylon is in crochet chain (Tess Marsh).*

right:
Fishing man. *Simple shapes in three basic knitting stitches, moss, rib and plain (Judy March). Also shown on back cover.*

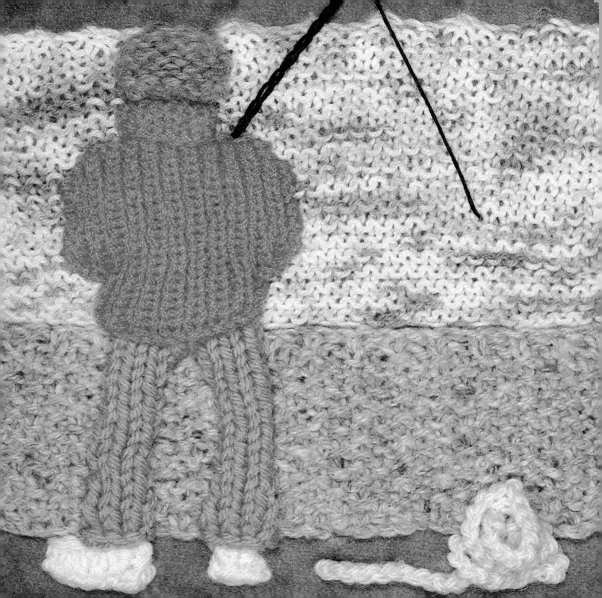

The knit stitch

Hold the yarn at the back of the work. Insert the right-hand needle into the first stitch on the left-hand needle from front to back, left to right as in Fig. 8. This is known as 'knitwise'. Pass the yarn round the right-hand needle point as shown in Fig. 9 and draw the loop through to the front of the work as in Fig. 10. Slip the stitch off the left-hand needle as in Fig. 11. Continue in this way along the row until you have transferred all the stitches to the right-hand needle. Turn the work and hold it in the left hand in preparation for the next row.

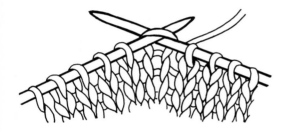

Fig. 8. The knit stitch

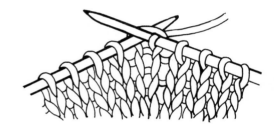

Fig. 10.

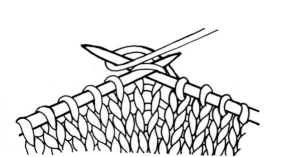

Fig. 9.

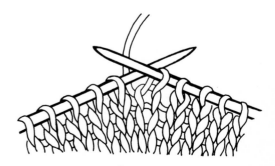

Fig. 11.

The purl stitch

With the yarn at the front of the work, insert the right-hand needle into the front of the first stitch on the left-hand needle from right to left as in Fig. 12. This is known as 'purlwise'. Pass the yarn round the right-hand needle point as in Fig. 13. Draw the loop through as in Fig. 14, then slip the stitch off the left-hand needle as in Fig. 15. Continue in this way along the row.

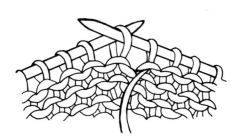

Fig. 12. The purl stitch

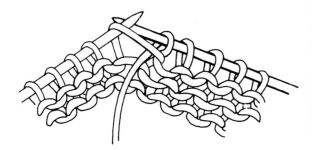

Fig. 14.

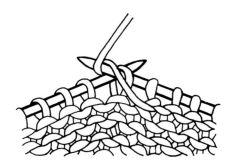

Fig. 13.

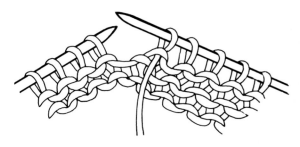

Fig. 15.

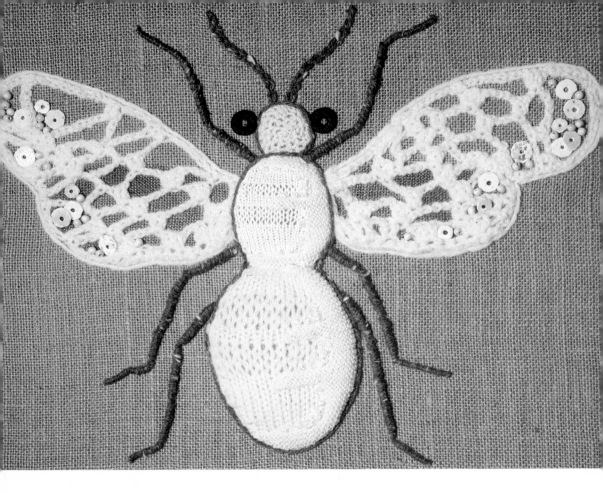

above:

Wasp. *The body is knitted on two different sizes of needle and two different knitting wools, highlighted with French knots in raffine. The wings are crocheted. The eyes are tap washers bound with wool, and the legs are cord whipped with wool. Couching is used round the wings and beads added (Beryl Court).*

right:

Pink cherry tree. *The tree is worked in stocking stitch and garter stitch, with mohair and double knitting wool. French knots are used at the base of the trunk. The loops are made by winding the yarn two or more times round the needle when making the stitch, and knitting only one loop of each stitch on the following row, so that the number of stitches remains the same (Penny Cuthbert).*

8

Casting off

Work casting off using all knit stitches or all purl stitches but on a ribbed fabric (see page 12) work knit and purl stitches alternately to maintain the pattern and, therefore, its elasticity.

Work the first two stitches in the usual way. Insert the point of the left-hand needle into the first of these stitches and, lifting it over the second one, slip it off the needle, as in Fig. 16.

Work another stitch and pass the previous one over it and off the needle as before. Continue in this way to the end of the row until only one stitch remains. Cut the yarn and pass the end through this last stitch, drawing it tight to fasten off.

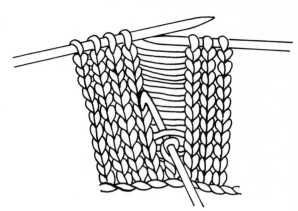

Fig. 17. Picking up a dropped stitch

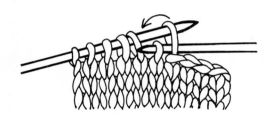

Fig. 16. Casting off

Dropped stitches

It is very easy, especially for a beginner, to drop a stitch, i.e., to let it slip off the needle unintentionally causing a ladder down several rows.

To pick it up again, insert a crochet hook into the loop from front to back and draw the first thread of the ladder above it through the loop to the front of the work, as shown in Fig. 17. Draw the next thread of the ladder through this new loop and so on to the top when the stitch is returned safely to the needle. For knit stitches, work from the front and for purl stitches from the back.

Tension

Tension is the name given to the number of stitches and rows required to achieve a certain measurement, using a specified yarn on a specified needle size. A designer uses this information to work out how many stitches and rows are required to make a garment to the correct size and it is, therefore, vital that you achieve the same tension or your garment will not fit.

Never begin to make anything without first working a sample of at least 10 cm (4 in.) square, using the recommended needle size. Lay the sample on a firm flat surface and using a ruler mark the measurement given in the tension with pins as shown in Fig. 18. Count the number of stitches or rows between the pins. If this is not the same as the instructions specify, make another square using a different size of needles. If you have too many stitches and rows try a larger size of needles, if too few, a smaller size. A tension check is always worth the time spent on it. Even a difference of half a stitch can be sufficient to add or subtract a great deal over the whole garment and you could end up with a completely different size from the one you want.

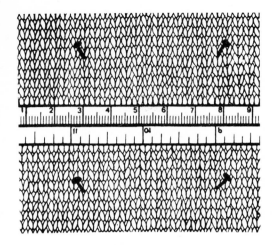
Fig. 18. How to measure tension

Simple stitch patterns

Even with only the basic information given so far it is already possible to achieve quite a wide variety of patterns. Four of the simple stitches are garter stitch, stocking stitch, rib and moss stitch.

Garter stitch
Work each row entirely in knit stitches. The fabric is reversible.

Stocking stitch
Work one row knit, one row purl throughout. The smooth 'knit side' is the right side although reversed stocking stitch, using the purl side as the right side, is a recognized pattern, especially in tweed-type yarns.

Rib
Alternate knit and purl stitches across the row. The result is a reversible, elastic fabric – the reverse side of a knit stitch being purl and vice versa. Numerically, the rib can vary endlessly although a one by one rib (knit one, purl one throughout) is more elastic than, for example, a four by two rib; but a stitch knitted on one side of the work will be purled on the return row on the other side of the work.

Moss stitch
This is like a rib gone wrong. Alternate knit and purl stitches across the row and vertically so that a knit stitch on one side is also knitted on the reverse side.

Variations on the theme

In certain circumstances, usually stated in the instructions, a stitch whether knit or purl has to be worked slightly differently from the basic technique.
1) To knit or purl a stitch *through the back of the loop*, insert the needle and complete the stitch in the usual way, as in Figs. 19 and 20. This can be done to individual stitches for special effects, or to every stitch for a textured finish and a tighter fabric.

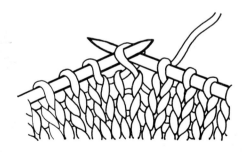
Fig. 19. The knit stitch through the back of the loop

page 12:
Sample stitches. *Top left, garter stitch; top right, stocking stitch; lower left, 1 by 1 rib; lower right, moss stitch.*

page 13:
Beige landscape.

11

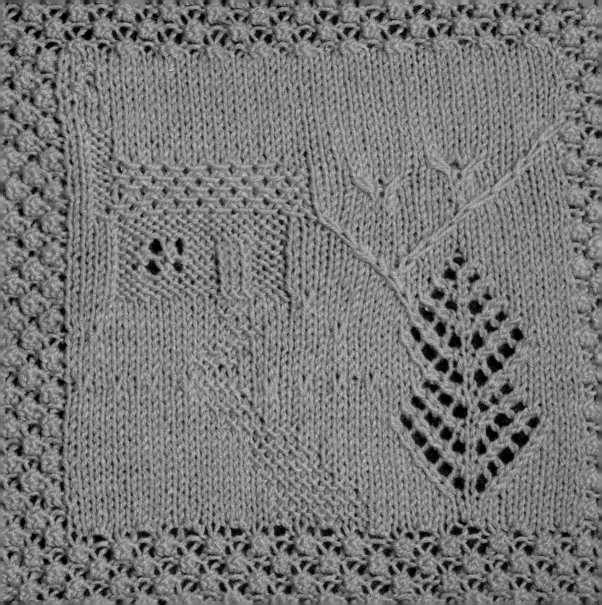

Fig. 20. *The purl stitch through the back of the loop*

Place this loop on to the left-hand needle, and knit or purl into the back. If two or more stitches are to be added to the end of the row then they are cast on.

Decreasing
The most commonly used method is to knit or purl two stitches together. Alternatively, a larger number can be decreased by casting off.

2) To knit or purl two or more stitches *together* as if they were one stitch, insert the needle through all the stitches at the same time and complete in the usual way.

3) To *slip* a stitch, insert the needle purl-wise, on both knit or purl stitches, and transfer it from the left-hand needle to the right-hand one without winding the yarn round.

4) To *pass one stitch over* another, once the two stitches have been worked, take the left-hand needle point and insert it into the first stitch, lift it over the second and off the needle.

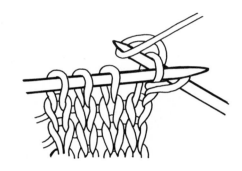

Fig. 21. *Increasing, first method*

Shaping

There are several ways to increase or decrease the number of stitches. Shaping can come at the ends of or within a row. Decorative methods are usually given in detail in pattern instructions.

Increasing
The most commonly used method is to work into the front and back of the same stitch. Do this at either the ends of the row as shown in Fig. 21 or within it.

An alternative method of increasing within the row is to pick up the thread which lies between the stitch just worked and the next one as shown in Fig. 22.

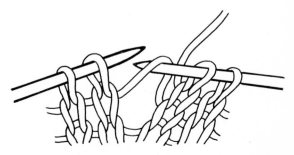

Fig. 22. *Increasing, second method*

14

Working in the round

If, instead of working backwards and forwards in rows, the knitting continues in a circle, the result is a tube and for articles such as polo necks, gloves or socks this does away with the need for seams. Whole garments are knitted this way, for instance the traditional seamless fisherman's guernsey.

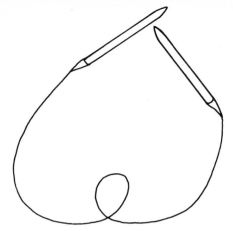

Fig. 24. Using a circular needle

When working in the round with a circular needle, it helps to have a marker loop in a contrasting colour to show the beginning of the round. Using a small length of yarn, make a loop and slip it on to the needle at the beginning of the round as in Fig. 25. Each time you come to the marker simply slip it onto the right-hand point so that it travels up the work.

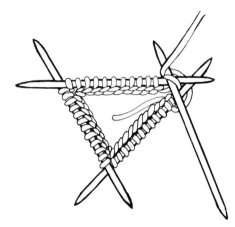

Fig. 23. Using four needles

There are two ways of working in the round: by using four needles with points at both ends as in Fig. 23, or with a circular needle as in Fig 24. Generally speaking, use four needles for smaller numbers of stitches and circular needles for larger numbers. To work with four needles, distribute the stitches evenly between three of the needles and use the fourth to knit. A circular needle has two needle points joined with a flexible length of plastic or wire and is useful for knitting a large number of stitches, straight working to and fro in rows.

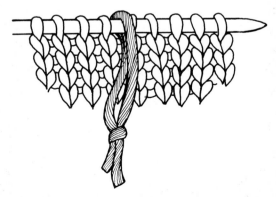

Fig. 25. A marker loop

15

Sample patterns. *Top left, quilted pattern; top right, wheatear rib; lower left, trinity stitch; lower right, lace pattern.*

Top right – simple 4 stitch cable twisting to right, 8 stitch cable chain, simple 4 stitch cable twisting to left. below; honeycomb pattern.

More complicated stitch patterns

Although these stitch patterns are more complicated than the previous ones given on page 11 they are still simple to do and are extremely effective.

A key to abbreviations is on page 26.

Quilted pattern
Work this on a multiple of 6 stitches, plus 3.
1st and every alternate row (WS) P.
2nd row K2, *yfwd, sl 5 purlwise, ybk, K1, rep from * to last st, K1.
4th row K4, *insert needle under loose strand and K next st bringing it out under the strand, K5, rep from * ending last rep K4.
6th row K1, yfwd, sl 3 purlwise, *ybk, K1, yfwd, sl 5 purlwise, rep from * to last 5 sts, ybk, K1, yfwd, sl 3 purlwise, K1.
8th row K1, *K next st under loose strand as before, K5, rep from * ending last rep K1.
These 8 rows form the pattern and are repeated throughout.

Wheatear rib
Work this on a multiple of 5 stitches, plus 2.
1st row (RS) *P3, ybk, take needle behind first st and K into the back of the second st then K first st and slip both sts off the needle together, rep from * to last 2 sts, P2.
2nd row *K3, yfwd, P the second st then the first and slip both sts off the needle together, rep from * to last 2 sts, K2.
These 2 rows form the pattern and are repeated throughout.

Trinity stitch
Work this on a multiple of 4 stitches.
1st and every alternate row (RS) P.
2nd row * (K1, P1, K1) all in the same st, P3 tog, rep from * to end.
4th row *P3 tog, (K1, P1, K1) all in the same st, rep from * to end.

These 4 rows form the patterns and are repeated throughout.

Lace pattern
Work this on an odd number of stitches.
1st and every alternate row (WS) P.
2nd row K1, *yfwd, K2 tog, rep from * to end.
4th row *Sl 1, K1, passo, yfwd, rep from * to last st, K1.
These 4 rows form the pattern and are repeated throughout.

Cables

To create a twisted rope effect, move the position of some stitches to cross either in front or behind other stitches. It is very simple to do this and requires a cable needle which is short and pointed at both ends as shown in Fig. 26. Use this technique to create an endless variety of patterns such as the traditional Aran jerseys.

To twist a cable to the left, knit to the first stitches of the cable, slip them on a cable needle and hold the needle at the front of the work, knit the next group of stitches and then knit the stitches from the cable needle.

To twist a cable to the right, work exactly in the same way, but hold the cable needle at the back of the work.

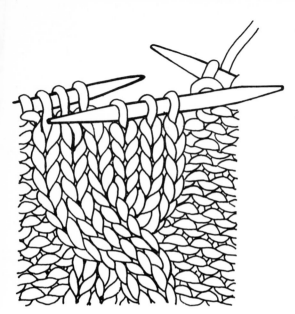

Fig. 26. Making a cable

Simple cables
Work this sample of simple cables over 28 stitches.
1st and every alternate row (WS) K4, P4, K2, P8, K2, P4, K4.
2nd Row P4, K4, P2, sl 2 sts on to cable needle and hold at back of work, K2, K2 from cable needle, sl 2 sts on to cable needle and hold at front of work, K2, K2 from cable needle, P2, K4, P4.
4th row P4, sl 2 sts on to cable needle and hold at front of work, K2, K2 from cable needle, P2, K8, P2, sl 2 sts on to cable needle and hold at back of work, K2, K2 from cable needle, P4.
6th row P4, K4, P2, K8, P2, K4, P4.
8th row As 4th row.
These 8 rows form the pattern and are repeated throughout.

Honeycomb pattern
Work this over a multiple of 8 stitches.
1st and every alternate row (WS) P.
2nd row *Sl 2 sts on to cable needle and hold at back of work, K2, K2 from cable needle, sl 2 sts on to cable needle and hold at front of work, K2, K2 from cable needle, rep from * to end.
4th row K.
6th row *Sl 2 sts on to cable needle and hold at front of work, K2, K2 from cable needle, sl 2 sts on to cable needle and hold at back of work, K2, K2 from cable needle, rep from * to end.
8th row K.
These 8 rows form the pattern and are repeated throughout.

page 20:
Sample stitches. *Top left, right side of stocking stitch stripes; top right, garter stitch stripes; lower left, 2 by 2 rib stripes; lower right, wrong side of stocking stitch stripes.*

page 21, left:
Sample patterns. *Top, stripes from a change in the yarn texture; left, stripes from a change in the stitch texture – stocking stitch and reversed stocking stitch.*

page 21, right:
Top, jacquard country cottage motif; below, Fair Isle border pattern.

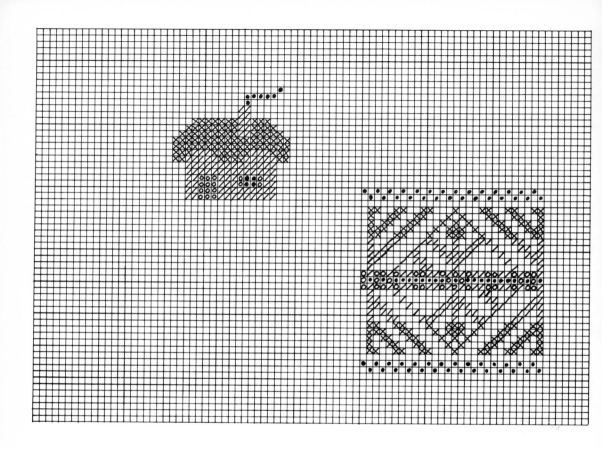

Key to jacquard country cottage motif

Background, beige	☐
Cottage and chimney, white	◩
Door and shutters, orange	◉
Window and smoke, grey	⊡
Thatch, brown	⊠

Key to Fair Isle border pattern

Oatmeal	☐
Dark brown	⊠
Mid brown	◩
Yellow	⊡
White	◉

Simple stripes

Create interesting striped patterns by simply changing the colour. For a regular horizontally striped pattern, use either an odd number of rows or an odd number of colours (with a minimum of three), so that the colour you wish to change to is available at the beginning of the appropriate row.

Horizontal stripes

Stocking stitch. Work the first row of the new colour on a knit row.

Garter stitch. Although this is usually a reversible fabric, to achieve an unbroken line always change colour on the same side. The fabric is then no longer reversible but the broken line of the colour change is always on the wrong side.

Ribbing. To make a smooth colour change, decide on a 'right' side so that the fabric is not reversible. Work the first row of a new colour in knit stitches only and return to the rib pattern on the next row.

Vertical stripes

As vertical stripes require a change of colour within the row at the point where the colours change, twist the two colours round one another before continuing in the new colour as in Fig. 27.

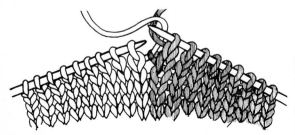

Fig. 27. *Twisting the yarns to link vertical stripes*

Textured stripes

Create a striped effect simply by changing yarns, rather than colour, or by using both techniques together. Here is a chance to be creative, but remember to check tensions and adjust needle sizes to give as near as possible the same tension throughout.

Complex colour changes

Using colours to make more complex patterns is called jacquard except when it is the very recognisable, traditional Fair Isle. Jacquard can have more than two colours in any one row. True Fair Isle never has more than two colours in any one row, although there may be more than two colours in the complete design.

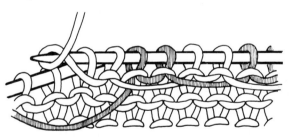

Fig. 28. *How to do stranding*

page 24:
Knitted sample. *Chenille, double knit, lurex and fine crochet thread in K2, P2 rib (Jan Messent).*

page 25:
Knitted sample. *3-ply wool and Bernat Klein textured wool knitted on no. 1 and no. 10 needles, with beads (Jan Messent).*

There are two methods of carrying the threads across the back of the work while not in use. The simpler is called stranding. Here carry any colour (or colours) not in use loosely across the back of the work until required, then twist with the preceding colour before using it, as in Fig. 28.

In weaving, the alternative method, twist any colour (or colours) not in use at regular, short intervals with the colour being used. This is the better method when a colour is out of use for more than three or four stitches at a time. The result is, however, a thicker fabric that uses more yarn, as in Fig. 29.

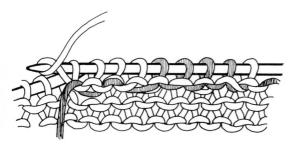

Fig. 29. How to do weaving

Following a pattern

When buying yarn, always make sure you have enough to complete the project in the same dye lot. Even a slight difference in the shade shows up remarkably clearly in a block of knitting.

Avoid substituting another yarn for the one recommended. Even two different 4-plys will not necessarily knit up the same so you may have difficulty in achieving the correct tension. Remember that when it comes to quantities, two balls of the same brand will not necessarily give exactly the same length of yarn and differing brands can vary even more. All sorts of things can alter the length even if the weight is the same: dye, for instance, can vary in composition

and some colours are more readily absorbed by the fibres – red always weighs more than the same wool in a lighter colour. Always check your tension before you begin (see page 10).

Follow the instructions in the sequence they are given. There is often a very good reason which you may discover too late if you deviate.

If the pattern is complicated, lay a ruler under the line of type you are working from. Keep notes of where you are, particularly in pattern repeats and when you put your knitting away.

You can imagine how lengthy instructions would be if written out in full all the time. Abbreviations are fairly universal. However, always check the abbreviations list; different publishers may mean different things by the same abbreviation.

Here is a typical list of abbreviations:
alt – alternately
beg – beginning
cm – centimetre
dec – decrease
g st – garter stitch
in – inch(es)
inc – increase
K – knit
patt – pattern
psso – pass the slipped stitch over
p – purl
rem – remaining
rep – repeat
RS – right side
sl – slip
st(s) – stitch(es)
st st – stocking stitch
tbl – through the back of the loop
tog – together
WS – wrong side
ybk – yarn back
yfwd – yarn forward

A square bracket usually contains the figure for the larger sizes so make sure you follow the same set of figures throughout. Round brackets generally group several details together and whatever immediately follows the bracket applies to everything within it. For example, (K1, P6) 6 times means repeat the instructions in the brackets six times making forty-two stitches in all.

Making up

Darning in ends
Join a new ball at the end of a row and always leave reasonably long ends of yarn. This allows you to darn them in securely when the knitting is complete so that they will not work loose. Using a blunt-ended needle, darn in each end along the edge of the work.

Blocking and pressing
Take care to check on the ball-band whether the yarn can be pressed – some man-made fibres are ruined by pressing.

Block or press the different sections of the garment before sewing them together. Pin each section out to size on a firm surface such as an ironing board or folded sheet.

Blocking. Simply lay a damp cloth over the knitting and leave until completely dry.

Pressing. Lay a damp cloth over the work and gently lower a warm iron on to it and press. *Lift* the iron and press down on the next piece of the work; *do not* move the iron across its surface.

Seaming
Different types of seams have different uses in making up. Whatever seam you use, always work with a blunt-ended needle and take care not to split the stitches.

Back stitch seam. A simple back stitch seam is best when the seam is across the grain of the fabric as along a shaped edge, for instance on a shoulderline as in Fig. 30.

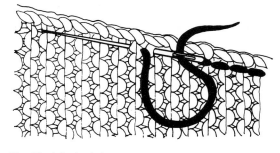

Fig. 30. A back stitch seam

page 28:
Knitted sample. *Stocking stitch stripes interlaced, using thick crochet cotton, 3-ply wool, mohair, and lurex thread on 3.25 mm (no. 13) needles. Add textured wool to the background for effect (Jan Messent).*

page 29:
Finger puppets.

Flat seam. To avoid bulk on ribbing or when joining on a button band, use a flat seam. Place the edges right sides together and secure the yarn. Pass the wool needle through the first edge stitch and straight through to the first edge stitch on the other side. Return the needle through the next edge stitches, as in Fig. 31. Continue in this way all along the seam.

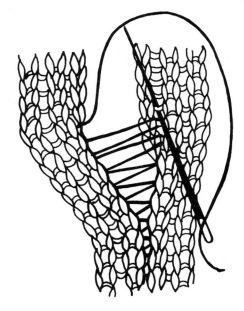

Fig. 32. An invisible seam

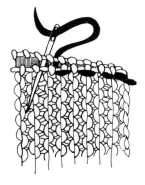

Fig. 31. A flat seam

Invisible seam. This is best used on vertical edges of stocking stitch. Place the two edges side by side, right sides uppermost. Secure the yarn at the bottom right, pass the needle under the thread between the first and second edge stitches on the first row, then pick up the corresponding thread on the left side of the seam, as in Fig. 32. Continue alternating in this way up the seam, drawing the edges firmly together.

Picking up stitches
To pick up stitches hold the knitting in the left hand with the right side facing and insert the needle into a row end (vertical edge) or stitch (horizontal edge). Wind the yarn round the needle point and draw the loop through to the front of the work, as in Fig. 33.

To pick up a large number of stitches, divide the edge with pins into equal sections. Divide the total number of stitches by the number of sections so that you only have to space the stitches evenly across one section at a time.

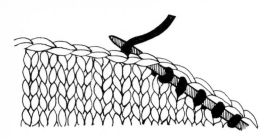

Fig. 33. Picking up the stitches

Finger puppets

Basic Pattern
Use oddments of 4-ply yarn.
Cast on 15 sts.
Rib 2 rows then continue in st st for 14 rows.
Work in st st for 6 rows★.

Shape top
Next row ★K2 tog, K2, rep from ★ to end.
Next row ★K2 tog, rep from ★ to end.
Pass wool through rem sts, draw up and fasten off.

Variations
The basic pattern can be made in stripes of two or
more colours, or two contrasting halves.

Finishing off
While still flat, embroider features, buttons, ties, etc.,
then sew seam down centre back.

Acknowledgments

Series edited by Kit Pyman

Text by Ena Richards. Drawings by Jan Messent.
Photographs by Search Press Studios

First published in Great Britain in 1980 by Search
Press Limited, Wellwood, North Farm Road,
Tunbridge Wells, Kent TN2 3DR

Reprinted 1988

ISBN 0 85532 428 7

Printed in Italy by Graphicom s.r.l.

Front cover:
Knitted sample. *Double knitting and bulky knit wools in stocking stitch on 3.75 mm (no. 9) needles, threaded with finer strips of knitting in 3-ply wool. Make the holes for the threading by K1, K2 tog. all along row, then, on the row above – P2, wool round needle to make one (Jan Messent).*

Back cover;
Fishing man. *Shown on page 5.*

Titles in the Needle Craft Series:

Appliqué (NC1)

Canvas Work (NC2)

Quilting (NC3)

Patchwork (NC4)

Smocking (NC5)

Stitchery (NC6)

Bobbin Lace (NC7)

Blackwork (NC8)

Embroidery Design (NC9)

Rag Rugs (NC10)

Knitting (NC11)

Machine Embroidery (NC12)

Spindle Spinning (NC13)

Drawn Fabric (NC14)

Patchwork 2 (NC15)

Crochet (NC16)

Small Scale Weaving (NC17)

Cross Stitch (NC18)

Machine Patchwork (NC19)

Goldwork (NC20)

Search Press also publishes the Craft Library, Leisure Crafts and Home-made Series and Leisure Arts Books.

Free colour catalogue will be sent on request.

Search Press Limited, Dept B, Wellwood, North Farm Road, Tunbridge Wells, Kent TN2 3DR, England